Through the Eyes of

CHILDREN

PERU

Connie Bickman

Published by Abdo & Daughters, 4940 Viking Drive, Suite 622, Edina, Minnesota 55435.

Library bound edition distributed by Rockbottom Books, Pentagon Tower, P.O. Box 36036, Minneapolis, Minnesota 55435.

Printed in the United States.

Cover Photo credit: Connie Bickman, GeoIMAGERY
Interior Photo credits: Connie Bickman, GeoIMAGERY
Map created by John Hamilton

Edited by Julie Berg

LIBRARY OF CONGRESS CATALOGING-IN-PUBLICATION DATA

Bickman, Connie
    Peru / Connie Bickman.
         p.   cm. -- (Through the eyes of Children).
    Includes index.
    ISBN 1-56239-325-1
    1. Children--Peru--Social life and customs--Juvenile literature.
    2. Peru--Social life and customs--Juvenile literature. [1. Peru-
-Social life and customs.] I. Title.   II. Series.
    F3410.B53   1994
    985--dc20   94-9905
                                                    CIP
                                                     AC

Contents

Introduction to Peru

Peru is one of the most interesting countries on earth.
You can live in a big city or a small village.
You can live in the jungle, in the highlands, or by the ocean.
Would you like to live by the Amazon River?
It is the mightiest river in the world!
Wherever you travel in Peru, the country and the people are different.

Thousands of years ago the Inca Indians lived in Peru.
They were a very advanced civilization.
That means they made many things that we don't even understand today.

Archeologists are still studying the Inca culture.
There is no written history to read.
Only mysterious art in gold, silver, pottery, and stone remain from the ancient people.

Machu Picchu is one of the cities built by the Incas.
The name means ancient peak, or old mountain.
The city is built on the top of a very high mountain.
How do you think the Incas could do this?
They didn't have big machines like we do.
It must have been very hard work.

Another puzzle is the Nazca lines.
They are huge pictures drawn on the desert.
They have been there
for 2,000 years.
The drawings are of
a hummingbird, a
spider, and other
animals.
They are very
mysterious because
they can only be seen
from the air.

Peru has deserts that reach out into the ocean.
It has beautiful sandy beaches.
Peru also has mountains that are sometimes covered with snow.
They are called the Andes Mountains.
People in the Andes speak Spanish and Quechua.
Many people also speak English.

PERU

Amazon River

Trujillo

Lima

Cuzco

Arequipa

750 miles

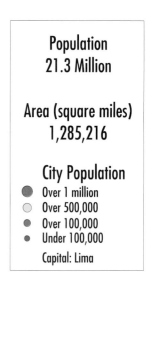

Population
21.3 Million

Area (square miles)
1,285,216

City Population
● Over 1 million
○ Over 500,000
● Over 100,000
● Under 100,000
Capital: Lima

More than half
of Peru is part of
the Amazon jungle.
There are many
tribes of Indians
that live in the
jungle.
They have many
languages of their
own.
Many also
speak English
and Spanish.

Millions of animals live in the jungle.
More than 1,200 different kinds of butterflies
live there.

Let's see what the children are like that live in Peru.

Meet the Children

As you travel through Peru you will see the children look different.
It is because they live in different temperatures.
It is hot in the jungle.
It is cooler in the mountains.
This boy lives in the Andes mountains.
His knit hat keeps his head warm.
His friend is a llama.

Many children live in the Amazon jungle of Peru.
It is far away from other people.
You can only find them by taking a boat and then
by walking.

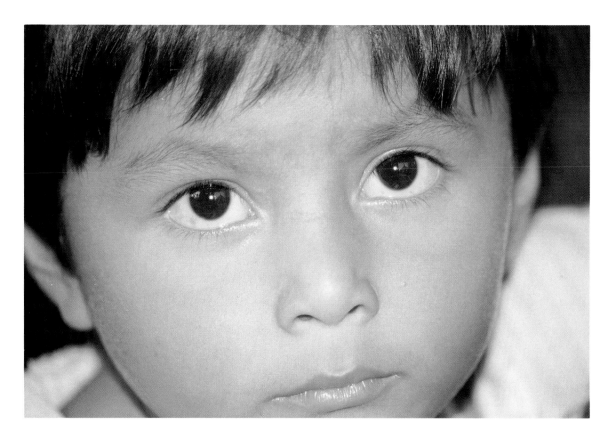

This little boy lives in a village on the river.
He likes to play games and to laugh just like you do.

What's Good to Eat?

Food is different depending on where you live.
In the jungle, most of the food is caught or grown.
In the mountains and cities, most of the food is
the same as yours.

Fresh fruits and vegetables are favorite foods.
This boy is selling them in the market in the city.

This boy is also selling food in the city.
Do you know what it is?
It is a beet.
People will eat it with relish or salsa.

Fish is a favorite food in the jungle.
Do you think the girl caught the fish by herself?
She did!

What Do They Wear?

Some children in Peru dress like you do.
Others dress very differently.

These people are in a market in Pisac.
It is in the mountains.
Do you see their colorful clothing?
Do you see the hats the ladies are wearing?
The different style of hats tell us what languages
the women speak.

These girls live in the mountains.
They wear many layers of colorful clothing.
When the sun comes out they can just take off a sweater.
They carry their belongings in a big cloth on their back.
The cloth is folded over and tied in the front—
almost like your backpack!

Where Do They Live?

Children in Peru live in different kinds of houses.
This boy lives in a floating city called Beline.
He can only get to his house by boat.

All of the buildings here are on long poles.
This lets the house go up and down as the water
rises or lowers.
Even the stores are floating houses.

Many houses are made of cement in the mountains.

Where it is hot, children live in wooden houses like this.

This is a jungle house.
It is called a tambo.
Do you see that it has no walls?
It only has a wood floor and a roof.
The roof is made from palm leaves woven together.
People sleep in hammocks in these houses.

The hammocks are hung from beams in the roof.
It is not so hot when you have no walls.
The wind can blow right through the house!

Getting Around

There are many ways to travel in Peru.
When you live in the jungle you need a boat.
Some people have motor boats and boat
houses.

These girls have a dug-out canoe.
It was made from a big jungle tree.
Do you see their pet chicken?
It is also riding in the boat.

People can travel by train in the highlands.
It is a beautiful ride through the mountains and valleys.

There are rivers and lakes to look at also.
This little boy likes to watch the train go by.

There are not many cars in the city of Iquitos.
People like to ride bicycles.
Bicyles are also used as taxis.
Three people can ride in the back seat of the taxi.

School is Fun!

Learning is fun wherever you live!
Like you, these children have desks.
They have books and a chalkboard.
They have a nice teacher.

These twin sisters are in class together.

Do you see the pictures of snow on the wall in this classroom?
These children traded pictures of where they live with other children who live in a colder climate.
Do you think children in the jungle have ever made a snowman?

How Do They Work?

Do you have jobs to do at home?
Children in Peru work also.
This boy's family has a sugar cane factory.
He helps them every day.

He picks sugar cane and squeezes the juice out.
Then the juice is cooked.
This boy is carrying the sugar cane on his back.
Do you see how he has a strap on his forehead?
It is so the load won't be so heavy on his back.

This girl is weaving. What do you think she is making? She is making a basket from palm leaves. She shredded the leaves apart to make the size she wanted. She weaves many useful things with the palm leaves.

Their Land

The country of Peru is beautiful.
As you travel from one end to the other you
will see many landscapes.
It is almost like being in different worlds.
This big city is Cuzco.
It is in the Andes Mountains.

These two boys live in the city of Lima.
They are visiting old ruins of Machu Picchu
in the mountains.
Peru has both mountains and jungles.

Animals are Friends

There are many unusual animals in Peru.
What kind of animals do you think these
girls have?
They are llamas.
Llamas like the cold weather and the high
land.

These girls have a pet in the jungle. It is a bird. They helped fix its leg when it was hurt. When it is better they will let it go.

Do you know what this animal is?
It is a three-toed sloth.
A sloth moves very slowly.
It likes to live in trees and eat branches.

Life in the City

Some cities are very modern with computers and big stores.
Other cities are large, but do not have a lot of modern ways.

This is a drug store.
It is the jungle pharmacy.
In Peru, many people eat the bark and plants from special trees.
They know what to mix together to make good medicine.
Many of your medicines are made from these plants and roots.

There are small markets in the mountains.
Many children help their parents sell their artwork there.
Visitors like to shop at these markets.

This is a big market in the city of Cuzco.
Here children help sell sweaters and blankets and pottery.
The stuffed llama would make a nice gift.

Family Living

Children help their parents work.
Children also help take care of their brothers and sisters.
This is a large family.
There are only a few houses in their village.
All of the people in the village are from the same family.
Sometimes many families live together in the same house.

This boy and girl are brother and sister.
They are also friends.
They help each other to learn in school.

These children are showing the beautiful jewery they have
made from seeds and things they found in the jungle.
The jewelry is very colorful.

They also have boat paddles made from trees.
And blow guns they use for hunting.

This family lives in the mountains.
Even though the sun shines bright
it gets very cold in the mountains.

These sisters take care of each other. They also help their mom and dad. They like to play games and have fun like all children.

What are Traditions?

Traditions are not the same in the jungle as
they are in the mountains.
That is because different kinds of Indians
settled in each place.
Each tribe had their own way of doing things.
These things were their traditions.
Weaving beautiful blankets and wall hangings
are part of the Inca tradition.
Many times stories are told in the weaving.
This girl carries her baby on her back in a
backpack made from a woven blanket.
The blankets are very colorful.

33

This boy is wearing a traditional hat.
It is paper, made from the bark of a tree.
He decorated it and added parrot feathers.
Skirts and other things are also made from
the bark.

Making jewelry and blow guns are traditions
in the jungle.
They are made from palm leaves, seeds, and
feathers found in the jungle.
Would you like a necklace like this?

Just For Fun

Children all over the world like to have fun.
These children don't have toys like you do.
They are making their own game with seeds
and plants.

Do you think it is fun to play with a llama?
The boys on the next page do.
They are taking care of a whole herd of llama.
They said it was not work.
It was fun!

Children are the Same Everywhere

It is fun to see how children in other countries live. Many children have similar ways of doing things. Did you see things that were the same as in your life? They may play and go to school and have families just like you. They may work, travel and dress different than you.

One thing is always the same. That is a smile. If you smile at other children, they will smile back. That is how you make new friends. It's fun to have new friends all over the world!

Glossary

Andes - mountain range in South America.

Amazon - jungle along the Amazon River, the largest river in the world.

Archeologists - people who study ancient history and people.

Canopy - umbrella of trees that cover the rainforest.

Inca - Indian people of the Andes. Ancient civilization of Peru.

Llama - a camel-like animal in South America. Its wool is used for clothing.

Machu Picchu - called "the lost city", an ancient ruin in the Andes.

Nazca - desert drawings called the Nazca lines are found near the town of Nazca.

Quechua - an official language of Peru.

Ruins - that which is left after a building or wall has fallen to pieces.

Tambo - a hut built of wood and palm with a floor, roof and without walls.

Index

About the Author/Photographer

Connie Bickman is a photojournalist whose photography has won regional and international awards.

She is retired from a ten-year newspaper career and currently owns her own portrait studio and art gallery. She is an active freelance photographer and writer whose passion it is to travel the far corners of the world in search of adventure and the opportunity to photograph native cultures.

She is a member of the National Press Association and the Minnesota Newspaper Photographers Association.

DAT

985
BIC   Bickman, Connie.

Peru

DATE DUE	BORROWER'S NAME	ROOM NUMBER

985
BIC   Bickman, Connie.

Peru